SHIT!

(it happens)

Crombie Jardine
PUBLISHING LIMITED

www.crombiejardine.com

Published by Crombie Jardine Publishing Limited
First edition, 2005

ISBN 1-905102-14-3

Written by Sara O'Melley
Cartoons by Bob Gibbs
Designed by 'Mr Stiffy'
Printed & bound in the United Kingdom by
William Clowes Ltd, Beccles, Suffolk

CONTENTS

INTRODUCTION

The Bible tells us that it rains on the just as well as the unjust, so it follows that into each life some shit must fall – let's hope not literally! Indeed all religions follow this code (see page 47). Yep, shit happens – to everyone at some time, although probably to some more than others, which may depend on whether

you are a negative or positive person.
Are you the person that thinks a pigeon
shitting on you is lucky? Or are you
the poor sod who was wearing the
suit he'd got out of the dry-cleaning
bag that morning? The *why-me?* kind
of guy? Well here's an overview of
shit and why shit happens, literally
sometimes, but mostly metaphorically.

LANGUAGE IS SHIT

No we're not joking here. Shit is a verb, a noun, an adjective. It's something we do, don't do, feel, talk, walk in, buy, look like, give, take, find, or lose.

Shit often has very negative connotations. Then again, if you haven't let one out for a while, shit can be a very positive thing. There is such a thing as good shit, you know? But in the main it's bad shit that happens. Anyway, shit permeates our language, and therefore our lives (and the whole of the house if you've dropped a particularly noisome one). If you're not following, here are a few shit examples:

💩 You're just talking shit.

💩 No, shit! *(Hold fire, as you wish, mate!)*

💩 You're shitting me, right? *(Why would I be shitting you wrong?)*

💩 I shit you not.

💩 That article has to be the shittiest

thing I've ever read. *(Except for the newspaper you wiped your backside with earlier.)*

💩 I bought some good shit today. *(It's all smelling of roses now.)*

💩 No shit! *(The phantom of the toilet is here.)*

💩 You shat on me then and you're shitting on me now, you crock of shit. *(Find a crapper, please!)*

💩 That piece of shit hasn't surfaced for years. *(Good flush system, then!)*

💩 Do you really think I did a good
job, or are you just giving me shit?

💩 I won't take any shit from
you, shit for brains.

💩 Give me some of that shit, will you?

💩 Do you want me to have
a shit fit, shithead?

💩 There's too much shit with
you around here. Get your
shit out of my house. *(Bucket
and spade in the garage?)*

💩 Do we have to sling all this shit about? The office should be a nice place to work.

💩 You really know your shit. You don't forget shit, do you?

💩 I feel shitty, Oh so shitty! I'm having a really shit day.

💩 She's shit hot, that new lawyer.

💩 He's been a grumpy little shit today.

💩 She's as happy as a pig in shit today.

💩 I wonder if anybody makes a shittier

mess than you, you dumb shit.

💩 You look like shit. Were you shit-faced again last night?

💩 I've got a mountain of shit to sort through.

💩 I'm up shit creek without a paddle.

💩 You don't give a shit about me, you piece of shit.

💩 You're so full of shit, you bag-o-shite. *(You need a crap.)*

💩 You've won, you lucky shit! What

do mean you picked different
numbers this week, you crazy shit?

 There's a lot of weird shit out there.

 I need to get my shit together
and get the shit out of here.

 Shit! I've just trodden in it.

SHIT HAPPENS TO BE . . .

Made up of water mostly, then of dead
bacteria, fibre, fats such as cholesterol,
inorganic salts like phosphates, live
bacteria, dead cells and mucus from the
lining of the intestine, and protein.

Nice stuff, hey? Of course no
two shits are the same – see
page 28 for types of shit.

SHIT RULES

If anything can go wrong, it will.

THANKS MURPHY.

SHIT RULES

- If there is a possibility of several things going wrong, the one that will cause the most damage will be the one to go wrong.

- If there is a worse time for something to go wrong, it will happen then.

- If anything just cannot go wrong, it will anyway.

SHIT RULES

- If you perceive that there are four possible ways in which something can go wrong, and circumvent these, then a fifth way, totally unprepared for, way will suddenly occur.

SHIT FAST

A passenger on an aircraft flushed the loo while still sitting on it and found his buttocks firmly stuck to the seat. It was only when the plane lost altitude that he was able to wriggle free. Moral of the tale, never flush with your tail on a toilet seat.

WHAT'S UP THERE DOC?

A 69-year-old man who was fed
up with the irritation caused by his
haemorrhoids, tried to relieve the
symptoms by itching himself with a
toothbrush. Sadly for him, he got the
brush wedged in his backside, and was
eventually forced to seek medical help.
His general practitioner was unable
to locate the toothbrush, however.
The man was given laxatives to try to
get him to pass it, but no joy there.
In the end it had to be surgically

removed. Supposedly, this was first and only time doctors have recorded a toothbrush being used in this way.

SHIT JOKE: NO. 1

While a man was staying in hospital, his bodily systems became extremely upset. Having made several false-alarm trips to the toilet, he decided the latest call of nature would turn out to be another one and stayed put. Shit's law, it wasn't, and he filled his bed with diarrhoea. Horribly embarrassed, he panicked, and, in a complete loss of composure, he jumped out of bed, gathered up the bed sheets, and threw them out the hospital window.

A drunk was walking by the hospital
when the sheets landed on him.
He started yelling, cursing, and
swinging his arms violently trying
to get the unknown things off, and
ended up with the soiled sheets
in a tangled pile at his feet.

As the drunk stood there, unsteady on
his feet, staring down at the sheets,
a hospital security guard walked up
and asked, "What the heck is going on
here?" To which the drunk, replied: "I
think I just beat the shit out of a ghost."

HOW S.H.I.T. 'REALLY' HAPPENED

In the 16th century, almost everything was transported by ship, including large shipments of manure. It was shipped dry, because it was lighter to carry; however once water got into the ship, the manure began to ferment, producing methane. Methane would build up, as the poor sod that went down into the bowels of the ship with a lantern in his hand would soon know about. BOOOOM! Several

ships were destroyed in this fashion
before people realized what was going
on. When they did work it out, the
bundles of manure were stamped
'Ship High In Transit', so that the crew
understood to stow it in the upper
decks. Thus 'S.H.I.T' came to be.

SHIT JOKE: NO. 2

One day two boys were walking through the woods when they saw some rabbit shit.

One of the boys said, "What is that?" "They're smart pills," said the other boy. "Eat them and they'll make you smarter." So the boy ate them and said, "These taste like shit!" "See," said the other boy, "You're already smarter."

DEFINING SHIT

- **The phantom shit**: a shit left mysteriously in the toilet that no one will admit to putting there.

- **The ghost shit**: you know the shit came out, but there is no shit in the toilet.

- **The no-flies-on-me shit**: it slides into the toilet in one go, disappears cleanly in a single flush, and there's nothing to report when you wipe your backside.

The wet shit: this shit, on the other hand, sticks. Not only does it leave skids at the bottom of the toilet bowl, the sort that needs a frenzied attack with the loo brush, but, no matter that you've wiped your bum twenty times, you still feel there's more to wipe. And rightly so, because later you'll probably find a skid or two on your pants.

The Kling-on shit: the poo where, when you go to wipe, it's still attached to your ring. A messy business that always happens when there's not enough loo paper.

➤ **The wet-bum shit**: the kind that likes to make a splash. Literally! It comes out so fast that your cheeks get soaked – usually when you're hovering over a dirty public loo.

➤ **The second wave**: this one happens when you've finished the job, pulled up, zipped up, left the loo and, oh shit! you need to go again. This usually occurs when there's a big queue outside the loo.

Not only do you have to hang on, but everyone knows about it, too.

The thunder blunder: basically, you go to poop and all that comes out is a tremendous fart; usually when there's someone in the cubicle next door. (By the way, a windy bum means an unhappy tum - change your diet.)

The here-to-stay shit: the kind where you strain so much you go bright red and practically pop a vein in your forehead.

The misfire: the kind that needs a map to locate the bowl. It prefers the seat, or the wall behind, and it's quite fond of the floor, too. Always happens when there's no bog-roll in town.

The something-died-in-there shit: this one smells really, really bad. Meat, eggs, onions, curry, beer etc. are big culprits.

The pizza-topping shit: it comes garnished with seeds, tomato skins, sweetcorn, raisins and the like.

The Oh-so-you're-back-again shit: you shit, you flush, it disappears, you leave, it hits the U-bend and comes back again - leading you to think there's a phantom shitter in the house, only haven't you seen that turd before?

The rainbow shit: now, before you panic, have you eaten beetroot recently? That'll turn your stools pink to bright red at any rate and may even look like blood. Some have said that eating lots of Kendal

mint cake turns your poo white,
while others have laid claim to blue
poo, green poo and black poo.

The chameleon shit: have you
ever observed that if you shit
in the woods it always comes
out the same colour as the
leaves you are shitting on?

The spinal tap shit: it hurts
so bad, you'd swear it was
coming down sideways.

The power dump: the kind that

comes out so fast, you barely get your pants down when you're done.

The fisherman's bobber: the kind that always happens in someone else's house. You shit, you flush, you flush again, but at least two pieces of shit are still floating and you have to conceal them with loo paper.

The frightened tortoise shit: it comes halfway out, then it goes back in, comes back out, goes back in, etc.

The crowd pleaser: this shit is so intriguing that you have to show it to at least one other person before flushing.

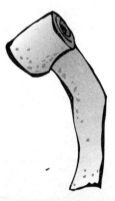

SHIT FACT

Floaters have an unusually high gas content. Sometimes the gases produced by bacteria in our gut don't collect into a large fart, but remain dispersed in the poop. As a result, this then has a lower density than water. Shit with a high fat content will also float.

GREEN SHIT CODE

As long as it is organic it's OK.

Recycle all shit as soon
as it happens.

Put your shit back into the Earth.

Don't burn shit, there's a shitting
hole in the ozone layer.

GOT THE BUMPER STICKER

'The audience of observers of bumper stickers is not made up primarily of minors or other persons of delicate sensibilities.' Georgia Supreme Court

In the land of free speech, many individuals have got themselves into trouble for using offensive language on their bumper sticker. According to David L. Hudson Jr., a First Amendment Center research attorney, James Daniel Cunningham was fined $100 in Georgia for having a bumper sticker bearing the words 'Shit Happens' on his car. The case went to the Georgia Supreme Court who in fact took Cunningham's side, because the 'profane or lewd' words he had displayed were not directed at a 'particular audience'. Similarly, in Boulder in the 1980s, anyone who had a bumper sticker stating, 'Shit Happens' was asked to take it off because it might offend people.

WEAR THE T-SHIRT

In the film *Forrest Gump*, a character steps on some dog poop, and Forrest observes, "It happens". This incident is supposed to have inspired the 'shit happens' slogan, but nobody seems sure who first originated the phrase.

BOG ROOM GRAFFITI

Everybody pisses on the floor.
Be a hero and shit on the ceiling.

Some people come
here to take a shit;
I come here to
leave one.

shit happens – look
no loo roll!

BUM FODDER

A lady was taking her daughter to London by train. She asked the child if she needed the loo before they left home. The child said she didn't. However, when they got to the local station the child had to have a poo, in the filthy station toilet. There was no loo roll and the mother used her pack of tissues to line the seat and for the necessary after wipe. While the mother was ticking off the child for not going before they left home, she herself felt the urge to go. She hung on, but by the time they reached Victoria Station she was desperate, rushed the child into the loo with her, and only after sweet release did she notice that, despite having to pay twenty pence to answer the call of nature, there was no paper in this loo either. Not feeling she could risk letting her child go and get some from another cubicle, she decided to use a page of the *Daily Mail* she had with her (anyone seen the ads. about the print not coming of on your hands? Well, that is true of bums too.), thinking this was a clever piece of improvision. However, on the return journey, mum got bored of playing I-spy and told her daughter she was going to read the paper. The daughter promptly announced to the full carriage: "But, you can't. You wiped you bottom on it!"

TOILET TRAINING

A City man had enjoyed a night out with the boys. On the train home he realized that he needed to take a shit and stumbled along the carriage to the conveniences. Unfortunately for him, in his drunken condition he didn't realize that the back of his raincoat was in the firing line, and that as he walked back along the carriage, he was also leaving behind a shitty trail.

* * *

RELIGIOUS SHIT

Agnosticism: I'm not sure about this shit happens business.

Atheism: I don't believe shit happens.

B.C.Creationism: And the Lord said "Let shit happen" . . . and there came piles of it.

Buddhism: If shit happens, it isn't really shit.

Calvinism: Shit happens

to people who don't work
hard enough to avoid it.

Catholicism: If shit happens,
you must confess to it.

Christian Science: Shit
happening is all in your mind.

Confucianism: Confucius
says, Shit Happens.

Congregationalism: Shit that
happens to one person is just as good
as shit that happens to another.

Episcopalian: It's not so bad if shit happens, as long as you serve the right wine with it.

Fundamentalism: Shit must be born again.

Gnosticism: I know why shit happens but won't tell you.

Greek Orthodox: Shit happens, usually in threes.

Hare Krishna: Shit happens Rama Rama Ding Dong.

Hinduism: Shit happens over and over and over until you're just plain pooped.

Islam: If shit happens, it is the will of Allah.

Jehovah's Witnesses: Knock, Knock, Shit Happens. May we have a moment of your time to show you some of our shit?

Judaism: Why does shit always happen to us?

Lutheran: If shit happens,

don't talk about it.

Methodist: It's not so bad if shit happens, as long as you serve grape juice with it.

Moonies: Only really happy shit happens.

Mormonism: God sent us this shit.

Mysticism: Just empty your mind and let your soul fully experience the shit happening.

Native American: What

is the medicine of shit?

Nihilism: No shit.

Occultism: Shit materializes
from other planes of existence.

Pantheism: It's all the same shit.

Presbyterian: This shit
was bound to happen.

Protestantism: Let the shit
happen to someone else.

Puritanism: S*** can happen all
day as long as you don't call it that.

Quakers: Let us not fight over this shit.

Rastafarianism: Let's smoke this shit!

Secular Humanism: Shit evolves.

Seventh Day Adventism: No shit shall happen on Saturday.

Sufism: The wise man never notices shit happening.

Taoism: Shit happens.

Unitarianism: Come let us

reason together about this shit.

Zen Buddhism: If shit happens in the forest with no one around, who will hear the sound it makes?

Zoroastrianism: There is an equal balance of shit and not shit in the universe.

SHIT, I'M SORRY GOD

- A religious fanatic in Michigan
  was hit by a truck while standing
  in the road holding a banner
  on which was written: 'The
  end of the world is nigh'.

- A boy in Luton was writing an essay
  on why he didn't believe in God
  when he was struck by lightning.

- A young man was golfing with
  friends when a thunderstorm
  approached. He jokingly,

and one might add rather
stupidly, dared God to strike
his golf club. God obliged.

- In Swaziland, nine people,
  including the priest, were killed
  when lightning struck a church.

BRIDAL WAIL

Everything was all set up for a wedding in an idyllic location when a storm blew up. The entire cocktail tent was blown over the sea wall, tables went over and the chairs and linens were blown out to sea. Meanwhile, the church got struck by lightning and the ceremony had to be held in darkness.

The Honeymoon's
Over Shit:

*any shit
deposited in
the presence of
another person.*

SCIENTIFIC SHIT

Applied Mathematics: The probability of shit happening approaches unity.

Archaeology: All we can dig is the same old shit over and over again.

Classical Physics: Shit does not 'happen', it just moves around.

Computer Programming: Should shit happen, just turn it off and turn it on again.

Computer Science: If shit happens, we'll fix it in the next version.

Darwinism: The survival of the shittiest.

Economics: Shit happens because there's a great demand for it.

Historicism: The same old shit happens again and again.

Quantum Physics: Shit happens but you can't say both where and when.

You wake at 7:00 a.m. every
morning but shit at 6:00 a.m.

A REAL SHITTY EXPERIENCE

A man had been constipated for some days and laxatives didn't seem to be helping – they induced a small brown trickle, but whatever else was up there was staying put. His stomach swelled up and, in immense pain, he finally went to his local A&E. After an examination he was given an enema. Again, out came a trickle, but otherwise it was no go. Time for the doctor to insert a hand up the bottom to remove the blockage, at which point Krakatoa erupted, spraying everything and everyone in the cubicle, and forming shitty silhouettes of the unfortunate medics on the walls. At this point a nurse pulled back the curtain, took one look and said, "Oh Shit!"

(AS RELATED BY A DOCTOR.)

SHIT JOKE: NO. 3

An Indian walks into a cafe with a shotgun in one hand and a bucket of buffalo manure in the other. He says to the waiter, "Me want coffee."

The waiter says, "Sure, Chief, coming right up." He gets the Indian a tall mug of coffee, and the Indian drinks it down in one gulp, picks up the bucket of manure, throws it into the air, blasts it with the shotgun, then just walks out.

The next morning the Indian returns. He has his shotgun in one hand and a bucket of buffalo manure in the other. He walks up to the counter and says to the waiter, "Me want coffee." The waiter says, "Whoa, Tonto, we're still cleaning up your mess from the last time you were here. What the heck was that all about, anyway?"

The Indian smiles and proudly says, "Me in training for senior management. Come in, drink coffee, shoot the shit, and disappear for the rest of the day."

SHIT RULES

The chance of the bread falling with the buttered side down is directly proportional to the cost of the carpet.

SHIT RULES

The legibility of a document is inversely proportional to its importance.

You will always find something in the last place you look.

No matter how long or how hard you shop for an item, after you've bought it, it will be on sale somewhere cheaper.

The other queue always moves faster.

FEMINIST SHIT

All men are shits.

All shit is a man's fault.

Shit need not happen to men;
men are shit already.

CHAUVINIST SHIT

What's this shit you're calling dinner?

We may be shit, but you
can't live without us.

SHIT JOKE: NO. 4

Sam dies and is sent to Hell. Satan meets him at the gates and shows him the doors to three rooms, saying he must choose one to spend eternity in. In the first room, people are standing in shit up to their necks. Sam says, "No, let me see the next room." In the second room, people are standing with shit up to their noses. Sam says no again. Finally, Satan opens the door to the third room. People are standing with shit up to their knees, drinking coffee and eating Danish pastries. Sam smiles and says, "I pick this room." Satan says okay and Sam wades in and starts pouring some coffee. On the way out, Satan yells, "OK, coffee break's over. Everyone back on your heads!"

YOUR DRIVING IS SHIT, SIR

10 REAL SHIT EXPLANATIONS FOR HAVING A CAR ACCIDENT

1. *A pedestrian hit me and went under my car.*

2. *I collided with a stationary truck coming the other way.*

3. *I was taking my canary to the hospital. It got loose in the car and flew out the window. The next thing I saw was his rear*

end, then there was a crash.

4. *Coming home, I drove into the wrong house and collided with a tree I don't have.*

5. *The accident happened when the right door of a car came around the corner without giving a signal.*

6. *I had been shopping for plants all day and was on my way home. As I reached an intersection, a hedge sprung up, obscuring my vision.*

7. *I thought my window was down;*

but found it was up when I
put my hand through it.

8. *The pedestrian had no idea which*
   direction to go, so I ran over him.

9. *I saw the slow-moving, sad-faced*
   old gentleman as he bounced
   off the hood of my car.

10. *To avoid hitting the bumper of the*
    car in front, I struck the pedestrian.

* * *

POLITICAL SHIT

💩 **Bureaucracy**: I don't care if shit happens as long as you fill out the forms.

💩 **Capitalism**: The more shit, the more profit.

💩 **Commercialism**: Let's package this shit.

💩 **Communism**: It's everybody's shit.

💩 **Diplomacy**: Let's pretend shit doesn't happen.

💩 **Liberalism**: Let shit happen.

💩 **Patriotism**: Better our shit than anyone else's.

💩 **Politics**: If shit happens, make a deal with it.

💩 **Racism**: White shit happens to me; brown shit happens to you.

💩 **Socialism**: My shit is your shit.

💩 **Tax Office**: Shit happens if you're on our shit list.

💩 **Military**: Attention! Shit will happen: HAPPEN!

SHIT JOKE: NO. 5

A woman goes to the doctors
covered in cuts and bruises.

"Christ," said the doctor,
"What happened?"

"Well," she said, "There was a knock at
the door and when I answered it a huge
grasshopper beat the shit out of me!"

"Ah yes," said the doctor, "There's
a nasty bug going round!'

SHIT JOKE: NO. 6

Sister Mary Margaret enters O'Flynn's liquor shop. "I'd like to buy a bottle of Irish whiskey", she tells O'Flynn. The owner of the store shakes his head and frowns. "A bottle of Irish whiskey? And you being a nun, too." "Oh no, no," Sister Mary Margaret exclaims. "It's for Father Reilly. His constipation, you know." O'Flynn smiles, nods, and puts a bottle into a bag. Sister Mary Margaret pays, takes the bag and goes on her way. Later that day, O'Flynn closes shop for the day. On his way home he passes an alley. There in the alley is Sister Mary Margaret. She's rip-roaring drunk, the empty bottle at her side. "Sister!" O'Flynn scolds. "And you said it was for Father Reilly's constipation." "It is," answers Sister Mary Margaret. "When he sees me, he's gonna shit himself!"

MORE REAL EXCUSES FOR SHIT DRIVING

In my attempt to kill a fly, I drove into a telephone pole.

I pulled away from the side of the road, glanced at my mother-in-law, and headed over the embankment.

I was sure the old fellow would never make it to the other side of the road when I struck him.

*An invisible car came out of nowhere,
struck my vehicle, and vanished.*

*The accident occurred when I was
attempting to bring my car out of a skid
by steering it into the other vehicle.*

*My car was legally parked as it
backed into the other vehicle.*

*As I approached the intersection,
a stop sign suddenly appeared in a
place where no stop sign had ever
appeared before. I was unable to*

stop in time to avoid the accident.

The telephone pole was approaching fast. I was attempting to swerve out of its path when it struck my front end.

The guy was all over the road. I had to swerve a number of times before I hit him.

And last but not least...

A truck backed though my windshield and into my wife's face. [Shit!]

SHIT RULES

Left to themselves, things tend
to go from bad to worse.

If everything seems to be going well, you
have obviously overlooked something.

Nature always sides with the hidden flaw.

Anything you try to fix will take longer
and cost you more than you thought.

If you fool around with a thing for

very long you will screw it up.

When a broken appliance is
demonstrated for the repairman,
it will work perfectly.

Everyone has a scheme for
getting rich that will not work.

There's never time to do it right, but
there's always time to do it wrong.

* * *

TOP SHIT

When the body was first created,
all the parts wanted to be boss.

The brain said, "I should be boss
because I control all of the body's
responses and functions."

The feet said, "We should be boss

since we carry the brain about and get him where he wants to go."

The hands said, "We should be the boss because we do all the work and earn all the money."

Finally, the arsehole spoke up.

All the parts laughed at the idea of the arsehole being the boss. So, the arsehole went on strike, blocked itself up, and refused to work.

Within a short time, the eyes became crossed, the hands clenched, the feet twitched, the heart and lungs began to panic, and the brain fevered.

Eventually, they all decided that the arsehole should be the boss, so the motion was passed. All the other parts did all the work while the boss just sat and passed out the shit!

ANIMAL SHIT

Bullshit: you are joking; you are having me on; it's not for real. *That story you just told me was bullshit. You were bullshitting all along.*

Horseshit: similar to bullshit, but with the emphasis on not being good or true. *That speech was utter horseshit.*

Chickenshit: used to describe a person who is cowardly.

He was too chickenshit to
go on the roller coaster.

Apeshit: is a state of panic or
frenzy, especially a sudden
or violent one.
When the parents found out
about the party on Saturday
night they went apeshit.

Ratshit: like rat-arsed;
severely inebriated, or
otherwise in a bad way.
After a long, hard week and

*a heavy night out, he was
completely ratshitted.*

Pigshit: not very bright. Usually used in the derogative comparison. *He's as thick as pigshit.*

Wormshit: lowlife. Usually used with reference to a lowlife person. *The little wormshit screwed up my holiday.*

Dogshit: the one that always ends up on new shoes.

* * *

SHIT JOKE: NO. 7

A turkey was chatting with a bull. "I would love to be able to get to the top of that tree," the turkey said and sighed, "But I haven't got the energy." "Well, why don't you nibble on some of my droppings?" replied the bull. "They're packed with nutrients." The turkey pecked at a lump of dung and found that it actually gave him enough strength to reach the first branch of the tree. The next day, after eating some more dung, he reached the second branch. Finally, after a week, there he was proudly perched at the top of the tree. Soon, though, the turkey was spotted by a farmer, who shot him out of the tree.

Moral of the story:
Bullshit might get you to the top, but it won't keep you there.

NO SHIT!

- Mel Blanc, the voice of Bugs Bunny, was allergic to carrots.

- The very first bomb dropped by the Allies on Berlin during World War Two killed the only elephant in Berlin Zoo.

- More people are killed annually by donkeys than die in air crashes.

- Walt Disney was afraid of mice.

READY, STEADY, OH SHIT!

Boyd Gittins, the American 400-metre hurdler, did not anticipate the event that would ruin his performance in the 1968 Olympic trials. Unfortunately for him, as he sprinted towards the first hurdle, a pigeon dropping hit him in the eye.

*

A 49-year-old San Francisco stockbroker accidentally jogged off a 100-foot cliff on his daily run.

ARRRRRRRR-SE!

In China, a tiger keeper was mauled to death when he climbed on the animals' cage, pulled down his pants, and did a shit. His body was found in the Bengal cage with his neck bitten and covered in blood. Police believe when the tigers saw his bare backside, they pounced on it and pulled him into the cage. Why he wanted to relieve himself in this particular way is unknown.

CAT SHIT

Firemen in Shropshire were called to rescue a cat from a tree. After some difficulty they were able to restore it to the arms of its owner. However, as they waved adieu, the cat sprang onto the driveway and, unseen by the engine driver, disappeared beneath its wheels. MIAOOOOWWWWWW!

* * *

DOG SHIT

A dog once ate a glove. He seemed fine and days passed and nothing happened to him. However, sometime later he had his morning crap, and out popped the fingers of the glove. The poor dog had to run about with a 'hand' sticking out of his bum until his next business trip.

* * *

THAT SOUNDS LIKE SHIT

"Who the hell wants to hear actors talk?"

H. M. WARNER, WARNER BROTHERS, 1927.

"We don't like their sound, and guitar music is on the way out."

DECCA RECORDING CO., REJECTING THE BEATLES, 1962.

SHIT JOKE: NO. 8

A lady walks into a Lexus dealership. She browses around, then spots the perfect car and walks over to inspect it. As she bends over to feel the fine leather upholstery, a loud fart escapes her.

Very embarrassed, she looks around nervously to see if anyone has noticed her little accident and hopes a sales person doesn't pop up right now.

As she turns back, there standing next to her is a salesman.

"Good day, Madam. How may we help you today?"

Very uncomfortably she asks, "Sir, what is the price of this lovely vehicle?"

He answers, "Madam, I'm very sorry to say that if you farted just touching it, you are going to shit yourself when you hear the price."

SHIT RULES

Anything good in life is illegal, immoral or fattening.

SHIT RULES

No good deed goes unpunished.

For any given software, the moment you manage to master it, a new version appears on the market.

Anything dropped in the bathroom will fall in the toilet. (Except sometimes a shit.)

The distance to your departure gate is directly proportional to the

weight of your carry-on luggage
and inversely proportional to the
time remaining before your flight.

If you want something badly
enough, you won't get it.

Any time you put an item in a safe
place it will never be seen again.

Your best golf shots always
occur when playing alone.

SHIT REVENGE

These are common revenge tactics. It's a strange world:

- Post a turd through the letterbox.
- Scatter manure in someone's front garden.
- Leave a dog poo in the front porch.
- Shit in your boss's desk drawer.
- Clean the loo with your enemy's toothbrush and replace it in the holder.
- Put laxatives in dinner.

Some farts
have lumps...

PHILOSHITTY

Altruism: Let all shit happen to others.

Fetishism: I love this shit.

Hedonism: There is nothing like a good shit happening!

Masochism: Please, please let shit happen to me.

Narcissism: Shit happens in my own image. I love my shit.

Nostalgia: Shit doesn't happen as often as it used to.

Optimism: Shit knocks only once.

Paranoia: I'm on the shit list.

Pessimism: If shit happens, there won't be enough for everybody.

Platonism: There is ideal shit happening somewhere.

Pragmatism: If shit happens, we'll find a way to use it.

Romanticism: Shit happened as she leant her wet cheek against him.

Stoicism: Shit happens.

Surrealism: Purple shit happens near melting clocks.

Utopianism: This shit does not stink.

SHIT JOKE: NO 9

Bill Gates, Andy Grove, and Jerry Sanders (CEOs of Microsoft, Intel, and AMD, in case you didn't know) were in a high-powered business meeting. During the tense discussions, a beeping noise suddenly emits from where Bill is sitting. Bill says, "Oh, that's my emergency beeper. Gentlemen, excuse me, I really need to take this call." So Bill lifts his wristwatch to his ear and begins talking into the end of his tie. After completing this call, he notices the others are staring at him. Bill explains, "Oh, this is my new emergency communication system. I have an earpiece built into my watch and a microphone sewn into the end of my tie. That way, I can a take a call anywhere." The others nod, and the meeting continues.

Five minutes later, the discussion is again interrupted when Andy starts beeping. He also states, "Oh, that is my emergency beeper. Excuse me, gentlemen, this must be an important call." So Andy taps his earlobe and begins talking into thin air. When he completes his call, he notices the others staring at him and explains, "I also have an emergency communication system. But my earpiece is actually implanted in my earlobe, and the microphone is actually embedded in this fake tooth. Isn't that neat?" The others nod, and the meeting continues.

Five minutes later, the discussion is again interrupted when Jerry emits a thunderous fart. He looks up at

the others staring at him and says,
"Uhh, somebody get me a piece of
paper . . . I'm receiving a fax."

PHILOSOPHICAL SHIT

I shit,
therefore I am.

Shit doesn't
happen; shit IS.

THE SHIT'S GONNA HIT

An airline hit on a very effective marketing promotion: Buy a first-class ticket, the wife goes free! Later they contacted the wives who had received free flights. However, eighty-five per cent of them knew nothing about the offer, while most had never travelled first class.

SHIT JOKE: NO. 10

Two guys are in a locker room when one guy notices the other guy has a cork in his arse. He asks, "How did you get a cork in your ass?" The other guy explains, "I was walking along the beach and I tripped over a lamp. There was a puff of smoke, and then a genie appeared and said that I had ten seconds to wish for anything I desired."

"What did you say?"

"No shit!"

MAY THE SHIT BE WITH YOU

Remember . . .

- It may be that your sole purpose in life is simply to serve as a warning to others.

- 'Shit!' is often the last word of English speakers who die in sudden or violent circumstances.

- The early bird gets the worm, but the second mouse gets the cheese.

◖ If you're not on somebody's shit list, you're not doing anything worthwhile.

◖ Change is inevitable, except from a vending machine.

◖ Those who live by the sword get shot by those who don't.

◖ Smile . . . tomorrow will be worse.

* * *

THE BIG WIPE OUT

A novice skier was making her first ever downhill attempt. Unfortunately, she quickly lost control, gathered speed, and shot towards the edge of the piste, where she sailed through a tear in the safety netting and flew towards the back window of a car parked below. As the driver got out, the woman got in, coming to rest with a ski wedged in her backside and needing some stitching. Needless to say, it was some time before she could walk straight, let alone ski again!

SHIT FOR BRAINS

Miss A had her flat broken into and, on top of the other goods stolen, her purse was taken from her handbag. She reported the break in and was not surprised to receive a call shortly afterwards. "This is the police," the caller said. "We have found a purse with your address in it. Could you confirm the pin number of one of your cards?" Being upset, she thoughtlessly did so, and the grateful thieves skipped off to the cash machine.

SELL ME SOME OF YOUR SHIT PLEASE

Rolls Royce had to change the name of
its car the Silver Mist to the Silver Shadow
before entering the German market.
In German, 'mist' means horseshit.

In Italy, an advertising campaign
for Schweppes Tonic Water ran
as Schweppes Toilet Water.

Supposedly, in French, the Toyota MR2,
is pronounced 'merdeux' ('shitty'!).

A SHIT BY ANY OTHER NAME . . .

Off to lay some cable.

Off to post a letter.

Off to chase a rabbit.

Off to ride the porcelain bus.

Need to make a pit stop.

Going to check on the scones.

Mr and Mrs Brown are just dropping the kids off at the pool.

THE KEY TO SHIT

A man who dropped his keys in a portable loo became stuck in said loo while trying to retrieve them. He yelled for forty-five minutes before anyone discovered his predicament. Not only did the police have to dismantle the toilet to get him out, but also the toilet seat had to be removed from around his torso by doctors.

*

In Detroit, a 41-year-old man got stuck and drowned in two feet of water after squeezing head first through an 18-inch-wide sewer grate to retrieve his car keys.

FIT SHIT

An electrician decided that he needed to improve his fitness levels. Thus, he put together a home gym, including a punch bag suspended by a chain from the ceiling. Unfortunately the first time he punched the bag he got the shock of his life and died instantly. Turned out he had wired it to a power supply.

THAT'S SOME GOOD SHIT YOU GOT THERE

A man was pleased with the healthy state of the marijuana plants he was growing in his backyard. Unluckily for him he received a phone call from the local police station informing him that someone had grassed on him and that, unless he wanted to get busted, he should bring the plants down to the station. He complied, only to find he had been the victim of a prank call.

HIDE THAT SHIT

Some undergraduates enjoyed a game of hide the turd. Whenever a housemate did a good log, he/she would hide it somewhere and challenge the others to smell it out. Usually this was a quick affair, but one turd took weeks to be uncovered. It was only when the students got near the bottom of the tub of margarine that it reared its ugly head – they'd been spreading marg on their toast all that time. This game is a health hazard; if you housemates suggest it, move out fast!

SOURCES, CREDITS AND FURTHER READING

Many thanks to all my friends for wittingly and unwittingly offering the inspiration for this book. Almost all the stories in this book are true, but you can never trust anyone implicity, so an urban myth or two might have made it in. If you enjoyed this book, there is plenty of good and bad shit about shit on the internet.

Shite
Excuses

Find the excuse they haven't heard before

1-905102-15-1

£2.99

All Crombie Jardine books are available
from your High Street bookshops,
Amazon, Littlehampton Book Services,
or Bookpost (P.O.Box 29, Douglas,
Isle of Man, IM99 1BQ.
tel: 01624 677 237, email: bookshop@
enterprise.net. Free postage and
packing within the UK).

www.crombiejardine.com

Please send your
shit happens stories to us at
shithappens@crombiejardine.com.